Our Lives, Our World

Mexico

Chrysalis Education

Distributed in the United States by
Smart Apple Media
2140 Howard Drive West
North Mankato, Minnesota 56003

Library of Congress Control Number: 2004108806

ISBN 1-59389-226-8

Compiled and edited by Susie Brooks
Associate Publisher: Joyce Bentley
Designed by: Tall Tree Books Ltd
Photographic consultant: Jenny Matthews
Photographic coordinators:
Gustavo Prado, Trisha Ziff
Picture researcher: Miguel Lamas
Translator: Gustavo Prado

Printed in China

10 9 8 7 6 5 4 3 2 1

The Publishers would like to thank the photographers,
Ramiro Chaves, Martha Miranda, Fernando Montiel
Klimt and Pavka Segura, for capturing these wonderful
children on film. Many thanks also to Gustavo Prado of
the Centro del Imagen, Mexico City and Trisha Ziff, an
independent curator, for their support and encouragement
throughout the project.

Corbis: Eric Crichton Front Cover(BL), 1(BC), 5(BL), Nik
Wheeler 5(TL); Getty Images: Cosmo Condina 4(BR).

Contents

¡Hola! — Hello!

We are the children of Mexico, and we can't wait to share our lives with you in this book!

Welcome to Mexico!

We've got so much to show you! Let's start by telling you a little about our country. We hope you'll come and see Mexico for yourself some time soon!

Our country

Mexico is part of North America. It is a long, fairly narrow country that stretches between the United States and Guatemala and Belize in the south. To either side of Mexico there is sea.

Popular beaches

The long coastlines mean that Mexico has some great beaches. They are very popular with tourists from all around the world.

A mountain capital

Mexico has lots of mountains. Some of these are volcanoes that still erupt sometimes. Our capital, Mexico City, lies among mountains in the south of the country.

National flag

The stripes of our flag represent hope (green), purity (white), and the blood of our heroes (red). The eagle is a symbol of strength.

The climate

Summers in Mexico are very hot. In the north, winters are much cooler, but the south stays warm and humid. There is a rainy season that lasts from around June to October. Sometimes, dangerous winds called hurricanes hit the coasts.

National flower

Our national flower is the dahlia.

Speak Spanish!

hola—hello

adios—goodbye

por favor—please

gracias—thank you

Sol

Hi! My name is Sol Peresvarbosa Maceira—my first name means Sun! I am 9 years old and I live with my mom in Mexico City. My pet dog is called Diente, which means Tooth. It sounds fierce, but he's really very soft and cuddly!

"My friends say I'm so funny. I'm always telling jokes and making people laugh!"

I really love my mom, Frida. Our favorite thing is watching cartoons together on TV.

My parents are divorced but they are still good friends. Dad lives next door. He's an artist and he paints here in mom's house.

This is our house. It has a big backyard and a great view of the mountains!

I go to school every day from Monday to Friday. Lessons start at 7:40 A.M. My favorite subjects are history and art, because they are the least boring!

Lots of herbs are grown here in Mexico. Doctors use some of them for medicine. We picked these ones on a class outing.

School days

Like most Mexican children, Sol goes to a large school for both boys and girls. She finishes around lunchtime and then has homework to do in the afternoon. Children in Mexico have to go to school until they are at least 16.

On Wednesday afternoons, I go to ballet lessons. Here I am with two of my friends, Florencia (left) and Alejandra.

I love to dance—I've been learning now for two years!

Sometimes I help to teach the younger girls.

"When I grow up, I want to be in a pop group or in the movies!"

On special occasions, a fair comes to our local square. I like playing marbles...

Spending money

In Mexico people spend pesos. Sol gets 10 pesos (about 60 pence) for pocket money every week, but not all families can afford this. Many Mexicans are very poor. Shopping in Mexico often means haggling to get a cheap price!

...and trying on earrings at the jewelry stalls. I usually try to save my pocket money, but I might spend some today!

The candy shop is another of my favorite places. I'm picking out traditional candies to take to a party at school.

These sweets are made from a fruit called tamarind, with sugar and lots of spicy chili. They are called "tarugos," which also means "stupid"!

Sweet celebrations

Mexicans love their candies and sweets. There are hundreds of different kinds—most are made from natural ingredients that grow here, including fruits, nuts, pumpkin seeds, milk, coconut, chili, and even cacti! Candies and sweets are popular during festivals such as Independence Day (September 15th/16th), when stalls and fairs are set up all around the country.

Toño

Hello! My name's José Antonio Camacho Cova, but everyone calls me Toño. I'm 8 years old and I live with my mom, dad, and brother in Cuauhtitlán, not far from Mexico City. Our home is in an apartment building owned by the government.

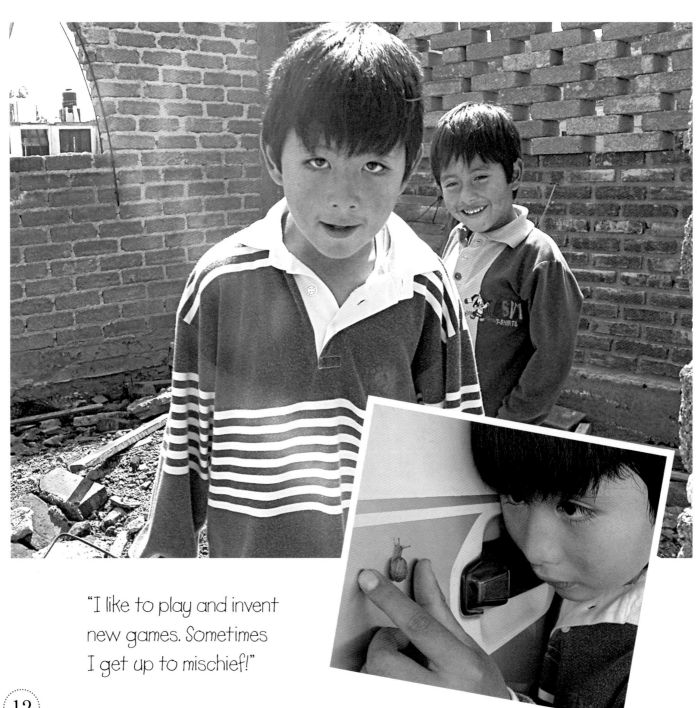

"I like to play and invent new games. Sometimes I get up to mischief!"

This is my family. My little brother Fernando is 6. Dad's name is Fernando, too! My mom is named Josefina.

Dad is a welder and an electrician. He also plays Mexican *salsa* music in a band. When I grow up I want to be like him—he's so cool!

My brother is my best friend—we're always happy when we're out messing around together.

Dad used to live in Xochimilco, a place built on canals to the south of Mexico City. I love to go there and ride on the colorful boats.

Sometimes Dad and his band rehearse their music here—I dance along! I'd like to play the drums, but everyone tells me I'm still too small.

We visit the local market to buy our food. We need some eggs, but Fernando and I wish we could take home a pet rabbit, too!

Amazing markets

Mexico's colorful street markets can sell anything, from crafts and clothes to live animals. They are popular places for food shopping. All kinds of tropical fruits and vegetables grow well in Mexico's sunny climate, so there's plenty of choice. Big red chili peppers, avocados, watermelons, oranges, mangoes, papayas, and pineapples are just a few of the things to buy.

There are so many delicious fruits to choose from!

My favorite festival is Day of the Dead. We get to dress up as ghosts and skeletons, and go around to our neighbors' houses asking for money and candy!

This is Fernando wearing his skeleton costume—spooky!

Day of the Dead

On November 2nd— the Day of the Dead—Mexicans take time to remember their relatives who have died. People visit family graves and set up altars in their homes, decorated with sugar skulls, photographs, and the favorite foods and belongings of the dead person. There are parties with music and feasts, to welcome the spirits of the dead back to earth.

At school we're all given candy skulls with our names on. We also eat special "dead bread," which has bone shapes on top!

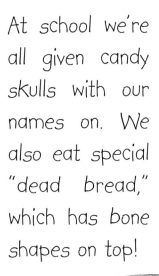

Saying prayers

Toño, like most Mexicans, is a Catholic. He believes in Jesus and the Virgin Mary, and he prays every night to God the Holy Father. Many Mexican children also pray to their guardian angel to look after them and keep them well. They make the sign of the cross when they pray.

When we go to the graveyard, we light candles, lay flowers, and say a prayer. This is my uncle's grave. I remember fun times with him.

Noemi

Hola! I'm Noemi Samara Galván and I'm 7 years old. I live in a tiny apartment in a government project called "Mermaids"—it's in Iztacalco, a part of Mexico City. My parents, grandparents, aunt, cousin, and brother all live here too!

"I love Mexico because I really like our food, our parks, our festivals, and our parties!"

This is my family, plus a couple of friends who live in the same building. Our home has only two bedrooms so I share with Mom, Dad, my brother, my aunt, and my cousin Fatima! My grandparents sleep in the other room.

Dad

Mom

Aunt Sairid

Gran

Brother Alfonso

Cousin Fatima

Mexico's people

Several cultures first lived in Mexico such as the Aztecs, the Zapotecs, and the Mayans. Later, they were joined by settlers from Spain. Like Noemi, most Mexicans today are "mestizos." Mexico's official language is Spanish, but there are also over 60 indigenous languages, spoken in many Mexican villages that still remain today.

Grandma is the most important person in my life. She is so full of love and teaches me all of the old Mexican songs!

Here we are outside our building. I'm not allowed to go far away on my own, but it's ok if Alfonso is with me.

"I like visiting the storytellers on the streets of Mexico City. We pay them 5 pesos to tell us a story!"

Sometimes we go to buy ice cream cones. My favorite is coffee flavor!

Most days we play outside with our friend Bryan who lives nearby.

We all like visiting the toy stalls at the local market. My dad and grandfather sell things here.

I also love to dress up! This is my traditional costume—it's from a place called Michoacan in the north of Mexico. I usually wear it on Mother's Day on May 10th.

Colorful costumes

Most people in Mexico wear Western-style clothes, but on special occasions they may dress in traditional costumes. These usually include brightly woven or embroidered fabrics. Shawls, rebosos (shawls for warmth and carrying babies), and wide-brimmed hats called sombreros are popular. In some indigenous villages, people wear traditional clothing every day.

My school is in the housing area where I live, so it only takes me 4 minutes to walk there. This is my classroom.

I start lessons at 2:00 P.M. and finish at 6:30 P.M. We wear a uniform with a tweed skirt, white shirt, and navy sweater.

Alfonso goes to the same school. Here we are with our headmaster. We don't often visit his office—but he's glad to be in this book!

After school we eat dinner. My auntie cooks all kinds of typical Mexican foods, including eggs with refried beans, cheesy quesadillas, rice, and belly of beef with chili sauce! We also eat tortillas with avocados, and other Mexican fruits for dessert.

Tortillas and quesadillas

Tortillas are eaten everywhere in Mexico. These thin, flat breads are made of corn, the country's main crop. Tortillas are usually wrapped around foods such as meat, beans, avocado, cheese, and vegetables. Quesadillas are stuffed tortillas that are baked and often served with spicy sauces.

Juan Pablo

Hi, I'm Juan Pablo García Miralrio—my last name means "look at the river"! I'm 7 years old, and I live with my parents and two brothers in Coatepec in the east of Mexico. I love my home, but I'd like to visit Mexico City one day, too!

"I'm happy and sporty—I know I am very lucky. I want to help the homeless children, because they have no food and no bed."

This is my family. My big brother Rafael is 14, and Xavier is 11. I share a bedroom with Xavier. He's always making me laugh with his silly jokes!

Dad is an architect. He built our house and most of the town we live in! Mom looks after me at home.

My naughty pet dog is named Coca Cola. She's wearing this bucket collar to stop her from licking a wound.

My friends all say I'm a little bit crazy! I like to play superhero...

...and mess around with my *bike*. It was so exciting when I first learned how to ride it without stabilizers!

Sometimes I hang out with my friends at the local park.

Fun and games

Soccer is by far the most popular sport in Mexico—both to play and to watch. Other sports that Mexicans enjoy include baseball, wrestling, and bullfighting. Dancing is also a popular pastime—traditional Mexican dances tend to be very fast and energetic!

"I've won medals for biking and for soccer, and certificates for doing tae kwon do!"

Football is my favorite sport—I'm a member of a local club. When I grow up, I really want to be a soccer player, because I love scoring goals so much!

We have some great toys in Mexico. These funny paper animals are called piñatas. They come in all kinds of shapes, and they're full of surprises! I'm choosing one for my birthday party.

Piñatas

Mexican children's parties almost all involve a piñata. It is a hollow model, usually made of papier mâché or cardboard, that is filled with treats, such as candies and small toys. Children take turns beating the piñata with a stick while they sing a special song—when it breaks, the treats fall out!

In Mexico we say it's the game that is important, not the toy. So we often play with simple things, like spinning tops and yo-yos.

Lotería is a little like bingo. A caller shouts the name of a card, or makes up a riddle about it, and you have to try to find it on your picture board. The first person to match a whole row of pictures wins!

I love these model wrestlers that we call "luchadores." I'm hoping to buy some more at this market stall.

Our Year

Here are some important events in our calendar!

Sol's birthday: January 25th

JANUARY

Three Kings Day Many people receive presents today instead of on Christmas Day. We eat slices of a special cake called "Rosca de Reyes," which has a little baby Jesus model baked inside.

FEBRUARY

Candlemass Whoever got the baby Jesus in their piece of "Rosca de Reyes" cake has to throw a party!

Flag Day We sing the national anthem and fly flags all around town.

MARCH

Birthday of Benito Juárez An official holiday when we remember the famous President who died in 1872. Around this date, we also celebrate the arrival of spring.

Easter school vacation: 2 weeks in late March/early April

APRIL

Holy Week/Easter We build up to Easter with parades, prayers, and parties. People break confetti-filled easter eggs over each other's heads!

MAY

Cinco de Mayo A national holiday in honor of Mexico's victory over the French who invaded in 1862.

Mother's Day We dress up in traditional costumes, dance, sing, and give our moms cards and presents!

JULY

Guelaguetza Oaxaca (in southern Mexico) hosts a famous two-week festival of dancing, music, and colorful parades.

Summer school vacation: 2 months from July 1st

AUGUST

Assumption Day An important date for Catholics, when we honor the Virgin Mary.

SEPTEMBER

Independence Day A huge festival celebrating Mexico's independence since 1810. The President rings a bell and shouts "Long live Mexico" from the balcony of his palace. There are fireworks, fairs, parties, feasts, and parades.

NOVEMBER/DECEMBER

Day of the Dead We make offerings, dress up and hold parties in memory of our dead relatives.
Posadas On any day between December 16th and 24th, we re-enact the Christmas story and finish at a party with piñatas and punch.
Christmas Day We celebrate the birth of Jesus.

Toño's birthday: November 1st
Juan Pablo's birthday: November 8th
Noemi's birthday: December 9th

Christmas school vacation: December

¡Adios! — Goodbye!

Glossary

mestizo A Mexican with mixed Spanish and Native American Indian blood.

piñata A hollow papier-mâché toy that is filled with candies and beaten with a stick until they fall out.

quesadilla A tortilla stuffed with meat or vegetables that is baked or fried.

refried beans Beans that are boiled, mashed, then fried.

resboso A shawl for warmth or to carry babies in.

salsa music A type of dance music that is popular in South and Central America.

sombrero A wide-brimmed hat, often made of straw.

tamarind A bitter tropical fruit that is used in cooking and in medicine.

tortilla A kind of thin, round pancake made from corn.

Index